TEKNON
AND THE
CHAMPION
WARRIORS

Misson Guide

AN INTERACTIVE ADVENTURE TO EXPLORE COURAGEOUS MANHOOD

A companion study guide
for *Teknon and the
CHAMPION Warriors*

A *Mentor Guide* for dads
and leaders is also
available

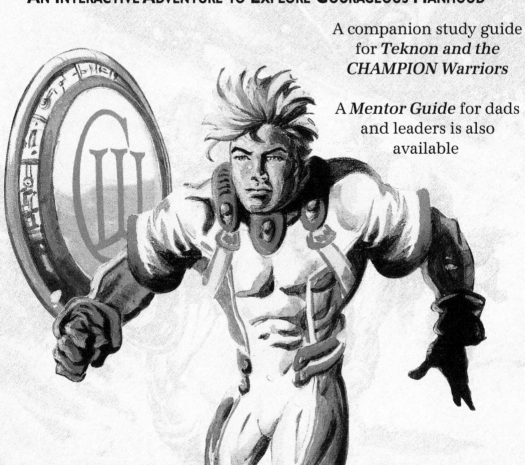

Teknon and the CHAMPION Warriors Mission Guide — Son

Published by Generations of Virtue
www.generationsofvirtue.org

Author: Brent Sapp
Editors: Megan Briggs and the Generations of Virtue team
Illustrator: Sergio Cariello
Designer: Generations of Virtue

ISBN 9780984896066
(previously ISBN 9780976614388)

Printed in the United States of America.

Most of the content of the Just Do It! appendix is taken from *Would You Like to Know God Personally?*, a version of the Four Spiritual Laws, written by Bill Bright. Copyright © 1965, 1968, Campus Crusade for Christ, Inc. All rights reserved.

Most Scripture quotations are taken from the New American Standard Bible.

© 1960, 1962, 1963, 1968, 1971, 1972, 1973, 1975, 1977, 1994 by The Lockman Foundation. All rights reserved. Used by permission.

The following Bible versions are also used:

NIV — Scripture quotations marked (NIV) are taken from The Holy Bible, New International Version®. NIV®. Copyright © 1973, 1978, 1984 by International Bible Society. Used by permission of Zondervan Publishing House. All rights reserved.

TLB — Verses marked (TLB) are taken from The Living Bible © 1971. Used by permission of Tyndale House Publishers, Inc., Wheaton, IL 60189. All rights reserved.

www.generationsofvirtue.org

The CHAMPION Training
adventure program
is dedicated to a pair of champions —
my mom and dad

TABLE OF CONTENTS

Vital Documents

CHAMPION Sessions

What is a Champion Warrior?

What comes to mind when you hear the word *warrior*? Today, that word refers to many things, like the road warrior who just invested his entire savings into an overpriced motorcycle and dominates the road. Or the weekend warrior, an overstuffed couch potato who sits in an overstuffed chair, watching whatever stuff is showing on TV all weekend long. And what comes to mind when you hear the word *champion*? Do you think of the guy who won several gold medals in the Olympics? Or the winner of the Indy 500? Those definitions may be true, but they bear little resemblance to the real warriors and champions of years past.

Many years ago, Native Americans living on the Western plains of the United States rode on horseback into battle when they reached their 14th birthday. A boy trained with his father early in life so that he could assume responsibility, take care of others, and, if necessary, fight to protect the safety of the tribe. These sons were more than teenagers; they were young men, each with the *soul of a warrior.*

In July 1776, General George Washington led his 5,000 troops, many under the age of 15, into battle against 25,000 of the finest soldiers Great Britain had to offer. Washington's outnumbered armed forces courageously held their position and played a vital role in gaining the freedom Americans enjoy today. These brave soldiers were more than teenagers; they were young men, each with the *heart of a champion.*

Since those days, many in our society have lost the vision for developing courageous young men. As a result, young men have not been given the responsibility they are capable of taking on. Many have not been challenged to think big thoughts and dream big dreams. How about you? Are you infected with the venom of low expectations or are you setting high standards for yourself? What are your values? What are your goals? Are you living a life full of challenge, adventure, and fulfillment?

How would you like to become a young man with the soul of a warrior and the heart of a champion? You can! Are you ready to begin the quest toward courageous manhood? Are you willing to invest the time and energy? If so, the CHAMPION Training adventure is for you!

Your *Mission Guide* includes 8 CHAMPION Sessions that you will complete and then discuss with your dad or leader over the course of several weeks.

Elements of a
CHAMPION Session

▲ **CHAMPION Characteristics:** One or two key character traits are highlighted for each session.

▲ **Power Verse:** A new Bible verse related to the session for you to memorize.

▲ **Discussion Topics:** Key subjects you will address in the session are summarized.

▲ **Reconnaissance:** Reconnaissance (or "recon") is also a military activity in which a soldier explores an area to gather important information for the mission ahead. In this section you and your dad will discuss an episode from Teknon and the CHAMPION Warriors.

▲ **Strategy and Tactics:** Strategy refers to the overall planning of a mission. Tactics refers to the methods used to secure the objectives planned out in the strategy. In this section you and your dad will discuss specific CHAMPION characteristics, investigate strategies and tactics from the Bible, and discover how to apply them in your life.

▲ **Main Things:** You and your dad will agree on some key principles and an action point you learned from each episode. You can record your action points on the CHAMPION Sheet of Deeds (located on page 9). You can work on applying these action points before your next session, and continue applying them as you develop these deeds for a lifetime as a CHAMPION.

Get ready for a challenging experience that will change your life!

THE CHAMPION
WARRIOR CREED

"IF I HAVE THE COURAGE TO FACE MY FEARS; HONOR, WHICH I SHOW TO GOD* AND MY FELLOW MAN; THE PROPER ATTITUDE CONCERNING MYSELF AND MY CIRCUMSTANCES; THE MENTAL TOUGHNESS REQUIRED TO MAKE HARD DECISIONS; PURITY OF HEART, MIND, AND BODY; THE INTEGRITY TO STAND FOR WHAT I BELIEVE, EVEN IN THE MOST DIFFICULT SITUATIONS; EFFECTIVE OWNERSHIP OF ALL THAT IS ENTRUSTED TO ME; AND FOCUSED NAVIGATION IN ORDER TO SUCCESSFULLY CHART MY COURSE IN LIFE; I WILL LIVE AS A TRUE CHAMPION WARRIOR, COMMITTED TO BATTLING EVIL, AND CHANGING MY WORLD FOR GOD'S GLORY."

* Note: In the fiction book, Teknon and the CHAMPION Warriors, the Warrior King called Pneuma is a fictional character intended to represent God (Father, Son, and Holy Spirit). For this study, the name Pneuma is only used when referring to the fictional story character.

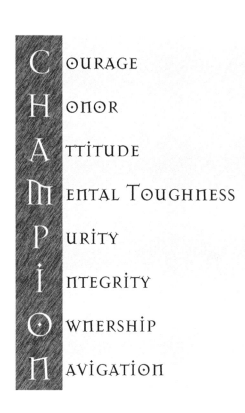

C ourage

H onor

A ttitude

M ental Toughness

P urity

I ntegrity

O wnership

N avigation

The CHAMPION Code

Character is the moral strength that grows out of our relationship with God.* Personal growth is expressed through the physical, emotional, social, mental, and especially spiritual areas of our lives.

Characteristics of a CHAMPION Warrior

Courage

I will cultivate bravery and trust in God. I will break out of my comfort zone by seeking to conquer my fears. I will learn to recover, recover, and recover again.

Honor

I will honor God by obeying Him and acknowledging Him as the complete source of my life, both now and through eternity. I will treat my parents, siblings, friends, and acquaintances with respect. I will appreciate the strengths and accept the weaknesses of all my "team members."

Attitude

I will cultivate a disposition of humility. I will assume a correct and hopeful view of myself as a member of God's family. I will improve my ability to manage anger and discouragement. I will develop and enjoy an appropriate sense of humor.

Mental Toughness

I will allow God to direct my thinking toward gaining common sense and wisdom. I will use discernment when making hard decisions. I will desire respect from others rather than compromise my convictions for acceptance or approval.

Purity

I will train myself to keep the temple of my body and mind uncorrupted mentally, emotionally, and physically. I commit to avoid and flee sexual temptation.

Integrity

I will seek to acquire a clear understanding of who I am in Christ so that I may have a deeper comprehension of what I believe, what I stand for, and how I can live out those convictions in the most difficult circumstances, whether I am alone or with others. I will allow other people to hold me accountable to standards of excellence.

Ownership

I will apply effective stewardship by using my life and the resources God entrusts to me—including my possessions, time, and talents—for His glory. I will seek contentment in God's provision for my needs. I will learn to practice delayed gratification.

Navigation

I will allow God to chart my course by accepting my mission from Him, and I will complete that mission by trusting in Him. I will study the Bible, God's Word, so I can know Him better and gain His strength and direction for my life. I will become goal-oriented by learning to focus my attention on completing worthwhile short-term and long-term objectives.

*Note: In the fiction book, Teknon and the CHAMPION Warriors, the Warrior King called Pneuma is a fictional character intended to represent God (Father, Son, and Holy Spirit). For this study, the name Pneuma is only used when referring to the fictional story.

The CHAMPION Sheet of Deeds

Following are my personal action points for each session of my CHAMPION Training. I will strive to apply these action points during my training adventure and also will make an effort to continue applying them as I seek to grow in godly character for a lifetime of living as a CHAMPION.

Episode 1: _____

Episode 2: _____

Episode 3: _____

Episode 4: _____

Episode 5: _____

Episode 6: _____

Episode 7: _____

Episode 8: _____

Episode 9: _____

Episode 10: _____

Episode 11: _____

Episode 12: _____

Episode 13: _____

Episode 14: _____

Episode 15: _____

Session 1:

Episodes 1 and 2

of Teknon and the

Champion Warriors

Episode 1: Destination: Kairos

Champion Characteristics

Courage and Navigation

Power Verse: Philippians 4:6-7

Be anxious for nothing, but in everything by prayer and supplication with thanksgiving let your requests be made known to God. And the peace of God, which surpasses all comprehension, will guard your hearts and your minds in Christ Jesus.

Discussion Topics

Prepare for a challenging task

Overcome fear of the unknown

Accept responsibility and trust God with the rest

Optional Exercise

Watch the movie *Iron Will* before this session. *Iron Will* is an excellent biopic about Will Stoneman, a young man who took responsibility to provide for his family after his father died.

Do the thing you fear, and fear will die.

Anonymous

Reconnaissance

1. Review the Map of the Mission on page 8 before beginning this section. Identify where the team is located in episode 1.

2. What is the CHAMPION definition of Courage? Of Navigation? (Refer to the CHAMPION Code on page 6.)

_____

_____

_____

_____

3. What is the team's mission on the planet Kairos?

Strategy and Tactics

Take Responsibility

In 1917, Will Stoneman gathered all of his courage as he stepped out of the train and into the frigid Canadian air of Winnipeg, Manitoba. He gazed for a moment at the bright lights and endless activity. At age 17, this rugged farm boy from the hills of South Dakota was about to undertake the greatest challenge of his life. In a few short hours, he would begin a 500-mile dog sled race in hopes of winning the $10,000 first prize.

Will needed the money to save his family's farm and pay for his college education. His father died in a sledding accident only a few weeks earlier, leaving the family without the income from their cabinet-making trade. Now Will was alone in a big city, about to race against the finest sled teams in the world over some of the roughest territory in North America.

What would most teenagers have said if they were faced with Will's challenge?

What can I do? I'm just a teenager.

It's too late for me to make a difference now.

Even if I tried, I'd probably drop out the first day, so I won't bother.

I don't have the experience. Why can't somebody else race for our family?

> *Success is peace of mind which is a direct result of self-satisfaction in knowing you made the effort to become the best that you are capable of becoming.*
>
> John Wooden, former Head Coach of UCLA - 10 time National Champions

Will Stoneman didn't choose to make excuses. He saw an opportunity to help his family, and he jumped at it. He took responsibility to compete in a difficult race, even though he had only a month to prepare for it. During that month, he worked as hard as he could, training himself to race on little food and even less sleep than any of his competitors. He did everything within his ability to contribute to his family's success.

Will's determination shocked the entire country when, against incredible odds, he won the race! His unwillingness to give up, regardless of the circumstances, earned him the nickname "Iron Will."

1. Read James 1:22-26. What happens if we only listen to the Word and do nothing? (See verse 22.)

   _____

   _____

2. What will happen to the person who takes responsibility to do what the Word says? (See verse 25.)

_____

_____

_____

```
┌─────────────────────────────────────────────┐
│                                             │
│   THE MAIN THING I LEARNED FROM             │
│           EPISODE 1:                        │
│                                             │
│   _____  │
│                                             │
│                                             │
│   _____  │
│                                             │
│                                             │
│   _____  │
│                                             │
│                                             │
│   _____  │
│                                             │
│                                             │
│   _____  │
│                                             │
└─────────────────────────────────────────────┘
```

CHAMPION SHEET OF DEEDS

Go to the CHAMPION Sheet of Deeds on page 9 and write down one thing you will begin to do before the next session (and beyond) to apply the main things you learned from Episode 1.

Episode 2:
My Enemy, Your Enemy

Champion Characteristics

Mental Toughness and Navigation

Power Verse: James 4:7-8a

*Submit therefore to God. Resist the devil and he will flee
from you. Draw near to God and He will draw near to you.*

Discussion Topics

Assess the enemy

Embrace your mission

Learn that God owns all things

Become an effective steward of your resources

Reconnaissance

1. Review the Map of the Mission on page 8 before beginning this section. Identify where the team is located in episode 2.

2. What is the CHAMPION definition of Mental Toughness? Of Navigation? (Refer to the CHAMPION Code on page 6.)

There are times when obedient acts of self-sacrifice and courage merit both admiration and profound gratitude.

William Bennett

_____

_____

_____

_____

_____

_____

_____

_____

3. In this episode, Kratos describes the team's primary enemy. Who is he and why is he so dangerous? What is he trying to do?

_____

_____

_____

_____

_____

4. What did Magos steal? Why did he steal it? Why did Kratos want to get it back?

_____

_____

_____

_____

_____

5. What is the CHAMPION definition of Ownership? (Refer to the CHAMPION Code on page 6.)

_____

_____

_____

_____

_____

6. Why did Teknon buy the Shocktech?

_____

_____

7. Did Teknon need the Shocktech? Why or why not?

_____

_____

8a. Was Teknon free to spend his money the way he
chose to spend it?

_____

_____

8b. Was Teknon wise in the spending choice he made?
Why?

_____

_____

_____

Nearly all men can stand adversity, but if you want to test a man's character, give him power.

Abraham Lincoln

9. What did Kratos recommend to Teknon about
spending money?

_____

_____

_____

_____

_____

Strategy and Tactics

Who Is Your Enemy?

Did you know that the Bible says you have an enemy? And did you realize that you should hate this enemy and everything that he stands for? Your enemy is Satan, also known as the devil. At one time, Satan was an angel, part of God's heavenly host (Isaiah 14:12-15, Luke 11:14-23).

But Satan became prideful and actually challenged God's authority. Like Magos, who chose to transform himself, Satan took matters into his own hands and allowed his pride to direct his actions. He wanted to become something he was not. He wanted to become God. As a result, God kicked him out of heaven forever.

When Satan was cast out, many of the other angels joined him in his rebellion. These angels now serve him around the world, which is currently in his control (1 John 5:19), by tempting, seducing, and enticing us to disobey God. Just like Scandalon is serving Magos, these angels serve Satan in his evil schemes.

Satan hates you and everything about you because he hates God. If you have invited Christ into your life, you are going to spend eternity with Christ in heaven. That is something Satan will never be able to do.

Satan's mission is to ruin as many people as he can. He wants to accomplish his mission before Christ comes back again to rule forever.

1. Read 1 Peter 5:8. What does the Bible say that Satan wants to do to us?

_____

_____

_____

2. How should we respond to Satan's plan for us?

_____

_____

_____

_____

My message to you is: Be courageous! ...Be as brave as your fathers before you. Have faith! Go forward.

Thomas A. Edison

Satan wants to infect our thoughts, our desires, and our actions so that we will be ineffective for God. If you are a Christian, Satan can't prevent you from going to heaven, but he can make your life ineffective and miserable if you allow him to do so. What's worse, he will use your poor choices, ineffectiveness, and disobedience to display you as a poor example of God's sons to the world.

But there's good news! God knows that Satan is your enemy. Your Heavenly Father wants to provide all of the strength you need to defeat Satan every day. Through Jesus' death, burial, and resurrection, He has defeated the devil (Genesis 3:15) and has overcome the world (John 16:33). All you have to do is put your trust in Christ and obey His instructions to be victorious.

3. Read James 4:7-8. What does the Bible say to do to the devil to make him flee from you?

_____

_____

_____

4. Why is it important for us to admit that Satan has influence in this world?

_____

_____

5. Should we fear Satan? Why or why not?

_____

_____

The Bible also says, "Greater is He [Christ] who is in you than he who is in the world [Satan]." You must realize that Satan is a formidable enemy, but you do not need to fear him. If you are a Christian, you belong to Almighty God, so He will give you guidance and protection. God also assigns His angels to us; they are charged with guarding those who fear and follow Him (Psalm 34:7, 91:11).

6. What can you do to protect yourself according to God's instructions in Psalm 119:9-11?

_____

_____

_____

Effective Stewardship

7. Is it wrong to spend money? Absolutely not, but God wants us to spend it wisely. Did you know there are more verses in the Bible concerning money than on almost any other subject? Why do you think there are so many verses about money?

_____

_____

_____

_____

Money is a tool God has given each of us to use and to manage. The way you manage money often reflects what you think about who provided it to you. Managing money is a visible expression of your relationship with God—your values and your trust in Him.

God is the owner of all good and perfect things on this earth. We are His stewards. What a privilege we have to be entrusted by God with His resources! God doesn't mind if you spend money. He may not even mind if you occasionally spend money on something you really want that you really don't need. But that should be the exception, not the rule.

Remember, God owns it all—our time, our talent, our possessions, and our money. He entrusts them to us. Think about what you buy before you buy it. Don't buy on the spur of the moment. Think and pray for wisdom before you make a big purchase. Seek wise counsel from others who are good stewards.

> *"Have I not commanded you? Be strong and courageous! Do not tremble or be dismayed, for the Lord your God is with you wherever you go."*
>
> Joshua 1:9

> *Beware of little expenses. A small leak will sink a great ship.*
>
> Benjamin Franklin

> *When prosperity comes, do not use all of it.*
>
> Benjamin Franklin

8. How can you become a good steward of your money and possessions?

_____

_____

_____

THE MAIN THING I LEARNED FROM EPISODE 2:

_____

_____

_____

_____

CHAMPION SHEET OF DEEDS

Go to the CHAMPION Sheet of Deeds on page 9 and write down one thing you will begin to do before the next session (and beyond) to apply the main things you learned from Episode 2.

Mental toughness • Purity • Integrity • Ownership • Navigation • Courage • Honor • Attitude

Session 2:
Episodes 3 and 4
of Teknon and the
CHAMPION Warriors

Episode 3: The Second Look

CHAMPION Characteristic

Purity

Power Verse: 1 Corinthians 6:18

Flee immorality. Every other sin that a man commits is outside the body, but the immoral man sins against his own body.

Discussion Topics

Understanding the right context for sex

Establishing boundaries in physical intimacy

Setting high standards to guard your purity

Reconnaissance

1. Recite as much as you can of the CHAMPION Warrior Creed from memory (see page 5).

2. Review the Map of the Mission on page 8 and determine the team's location in episode 3.

3. What is the CHAMPION definition of Purity? (Refer to the CHAMPION Code on page 6.)

_____

_____

4. Why do you think Scandalon tempted Teknon?

_____

_____

5. When should Teknon have returned to camp? Why?

_____

_____

_____

6. What did Teknon mean when he said, "I guess I shouldn't have taken the second look"?

_____

_____

_____

7. What did Kratos mean when he said, "Error increases with distance"?

_____

_____

_____

8. How does that insight relate to physical and sexual intimacy?

_____

_____

_____

_____

9. Why do you think Kratos suggested that Teknon wait until marriage to kiss a woman?

_____

_____

_____

_____

10. How did Teknon react to the idea of the Wedding Kiss?

_____

_____

Strategy and Tactics

1. Read 2 Corinthians 10:3-5. How can we win the battle for purity in our minds and hearts?

_____

_____

_____

2. Read Romans 6:12-13. What does God say we should not do with our bodies?

_____

_____

3. What does He say we should do with our bodies?

_____

_____

Just as Scandalon tempted Teknon, your enemy — Satan — wants to tempt you to fail in the area of sexual purity. If he can destroy your character, you are no longer a threat to him. Satan often uses sex to tempt us to sin. He sets traps for us and, if we don't allow God to control our desires, we'll walk right into them.

4. What does the Bible say about temptation in 1 Corinthians 10:13? How much can we depend on God when we are tempted?

_____

_____

_____

_____

God promises to provide a way out during any temptation we face. It may mean that we shouldn't take the second look. It will probably mean getting out of the tempting situation as quickly as possible. Remember, God promises to provide the power for you to live a pure life.

THE WEDDING KISS

Radical idea, right? But why not take every precaution possible to make sure that you will have the most fulfilling and intimate life possible with the wife God may eventually bring into your life? The world's approach to sex is not about creating more exciting and satisfying relationships, although the movie and music industry

Let us not lose heart in doing good, for in due time we will reap if we do not grow weary. So then, while we have opportunity, let us do good to all people, and especially to those who are of the household of the faith.

Galatians 6:9-10

I have been crucified with Christ; and it is no longer I who live, but Christ lives in me; and the life which I now live in the flesh I live by faith in the Son of God, who loved me and gave Himself up for me.

Galatians 2:20

would try to tell us otherwise. Sure the Wedding Kiss challenge sounds weird, but it's worth waiting for the benefits you'll receive in the long run. Kratos said that he wished someone had challenged him to meet such a goal. There are probably many men today who wish they had received a challenge like this when they were your age.

5. Read 1 Thessalonians 4:1-5. How do the Gentiles (non-Christians) behave regarding sexual activity?

_____

_____

> *Dear brothers, you are only visitors here. Since your real home is in heaven I beg you to keep away from the evil pleasures of this world; they are not for you, for they wage war against your very soul.*
>
> 1 Peter 2:11 (TLB)

6. How does God say He wants you to behave in this area?

_____

The idea of the Wedding Kiss is a brave and bold commitment to purity. It's holding on to the precious gift of your body and emotions until you can give that gift to one special person. People who choose to refrain from sexual intimacy before marriage will be blessed by God in powerful ways.

> *Walk by the Spirit, and you will not carry out the desire of the flesh.*
>
> Galatians 5:16b

7. What do you think your friends would think about the idea of the Wedding Kiss? How far do you think most teens will go physically with a girl?

_____

_____

8. Whether you go for the Wedding Kiss or not, you need to decide in advance how far you will go emotionally and physically with a girl before you are married. Have you ever really thought about how far you plan to go?

_____

You may have already taken a few steps toward the cliff that Kratos talked about. You may have kissed a girl, or maybe become even more physically and emotionally involved with her. If you have, now is the time to confess this to God and seek His forgiveness. Then, recommit yourself to a higher standard. Claim God's promise of forgiveness and cleansing (1 John 1:9), and start fresh today in this area of purity.

THE MAIN THING I LEARNED FROM
EPISODE 3:

_____

_____

_____

_____

CHAMPION Sheet of Deeds

Go to the CHAMPION Sheet of Deeds on page 9 and write down one thing you will begin to do before the next session (and beyond) to apply the main things you learned from Episode 3.

Episode 4:
The Company I Keep

CHAMPION Characteristics

Mental Toughness and Integrity

Power Verse: 1 Corinthians 15:33

Do not be misled: Bad company corrupts good character. (NIV)

Discussion Topics

Recognize the importance of discernment in choosing the right friends

Realize that there are always consequences to our choices

Recover from failure – part 1

Reconnaissance

1. Try to recite at least half of the CHAMPION Warrior Creed from memory (see page 5).

2. Review the Map of the Mission on page 8 and determine the team's location in episode 4.

3. What is the CHAMPION definition of Mental Toughness? Of Integrity? (Refer to the CHAMPION Code on page 6.)

Hold yourself responsible for a higher standard than anybody else expects of you. Never excuse yourself.

Henry Ward Beecher

_____

_____

_____

_____

_____

_____

_____

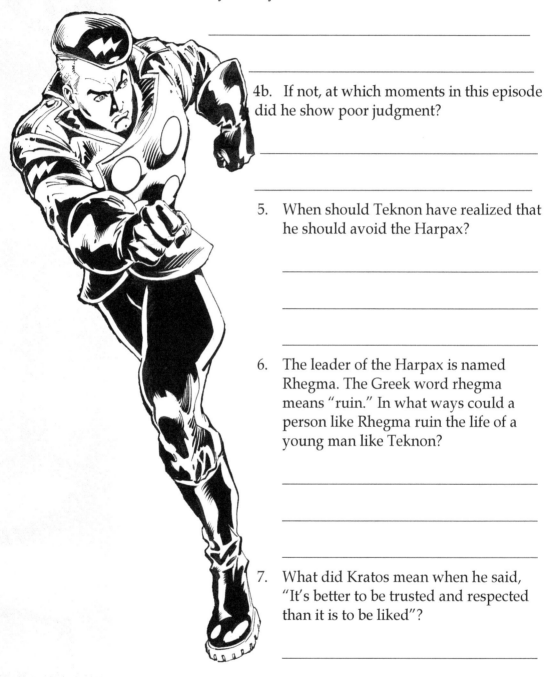

4a. Do you believe Teknon used good judgment in Bia? Why or why not?

_____

_____

4b. If not, at which moments in this episode did he show poor judgment?

_____

_____

5. When should Teknon have realized that he should avoid the Harpax?

_____

_____

_____

6. The leader of the Harpax is named Rhegma. The Greek word rhegma means "ruin." In what ways could a person like Rhegma ruin the life of a young man like Teknon?

_____

_____

_____

7. What did Kratos mean when he said, "It's better to be trusted and respected than it is to be liked"?

_____

8. Kratos also told Teknon that he must learn from his mistake and to recover. What does it mean to recover? How would you recover if you made a mistake like Teknon made?

_____

_____

_____

9. Kratos cautioned, "Observe all of the characteristics of a person." What characteristics should you watch for?

GOOD Characteristics

_____

_____

_____

_____

_____

BAD Characteristics

_____

_____

_____

_____

10. What do you think Kratos meant when he said, "Bad humor is a sign of bad morals"?

_____

_____

Strategy and Tactics

Most of the book of Proverbs in the Old Testament was written by one of the wisest men who ever lived, King Solomon. In this book, Solomon instructed his sons and the young men of his kingdom about the difference between knowledge (having the facts) and wisdom (applying those facts to life). Like Teknon, young men can choose to reject the wisdom of their parents and the Word of God. As they grow older, however, they will increase their knowledge, but not their wisdom and discernment. In Proverbs 1, Solomon described the danger of being a young man who lacks discernment.

1a. Read Proverbs 1. What can a person do to begin obtaining wisdom? (See verses 7-9.)

_____

_____

1b. What advice did Solomon give in verses 15 and 16 concerning the importance of choosing the right friends?

_____

_____

1c. According to verses 23-27, why should we listen to sound advice and wisdom?

_____

_____

1d. What will happen if we don't obey God and use discernment? (See verses 28-32.)

_____

_____

1e. What will happen if we use good judgment and listen to wisdom? (See verse 33.)

_____

Always remember two things about your Heavenly Father: God loves you and He is trustworthy.

God Loves You

Just as Kratos loved Teknon despite his bad decisions, so your Father in heaven loves you no matter what you do. He understands that you are growing and learning how to follow Him. Sometimes you will succeed, and sometimes you will fail. As you grow to know Him better and seek to obey His Word, you will increase in discernment and find it easier to make better choices.

But no matter how hard we try, we will still sin and disobey God. Romans 3:23 tells us that we have all sinned. God understands us and loves us so much that He sent Jesus to die on the cross and then raised Him again from the dead to pay for our sins (or failures). After we sin, we recover by confessing our failure to God and then claiming His promise of forgiveness. Then, we turn from our own way and go God's way. We should also apologize to anyone we have offended.

2. What does 1 John 1:9 say about God and confessing our sins to Him? How does this make you feel?

_____

_____

THE MAIN THING I LEARNED FROM
EPISODE 4:

_____

_____

_____

_____

_____

CHAMPION SHEET OF DEEDS

Go to the CHAMPION Sheet of Deeds on page 9 and write down one thing you will begin to do before the next session (and beyond) to apply the main things you learned from Episode 4.

Courage • Honor • Attitude • Mental Toughness • Purity • Integrity • Ownership • Navigation

Session 3:
Episodes 5 and 6
of Teknon and the
CHAMPION Warriors

Episode 5: Ergonian Pride

CHAMPION Characteristic

Attitude

Power Verse: Proverbs 19:20 (NIV)

Listen to advice and accept instruction, and in the end you will be wise.

Discussion Topics

The danger of pride

The importance of a teachable attitude

Listen to wise counsel

Reconnaissance

When a man is wrapped up in himself, he makes a pretty small package.

John Ruskin

1. Review the Map of the Mission on page 8 and determine the team's location in episode 5. Trace the steps the team has covered thus far. Review story highlights and main topics discussed.

2. What is the CHAMPION definition of Attitude? (Refer to the CHAMPION Code on page 6.)

   _____

   _____

   _____

3. What kind of attitude did Mr. Poroo have toward Kratos? Why?

   _____

   _____

4. What occurred as a result of Mr. Poroo's attitude?

   _____

   _____

5. What does the word "teachable" mean to you?

_____

_____

STRATEGY AND TACTICS

Life would be much easier if we were teachable, wouldn't it?

1. What does Proverbs 19:20 say about being teachable?

    _____

    _____

    _____

2. What happens if you are not teachable? (Read Proverbs 29:1.)

    _____

    _____

    Read Proverbs 16:18-19 and Proverbs 18:12.

3a. What kind of attitude creates the greatest barrier to becoming teachable and leads to destruction in the end?

_____

_____

3b. What kind of attitude makes us teachable and leads to honor?

_____

_____

God knows what is best for us. When we reject God's wisdom and direction in our decisions, we are trying to do His job. When we aren't teachable, we don't pay attention to God's Word. We also don't listen to people whom God puts into our lives to give us advice and counsel—like our parents, pastors, and teachers. We saw what happened to Mr. Poroo when he didn't listen to Kratos' advice. Make sure you are seeking God with a teachable heart so that He can reveal how to live your life for Him.

4. Do you think your friends (name a few) are teachable? Why or why not?

Read Proverbs 6:20-23

My son, observe the commandment of your father and do not forsake the teaching of your mother; bind them continually on your heart; tie them around your neck. When you walk about, they will guide you; when you sleep, they will watch over you; and when you awake, they will talk to you. For the commandment is a lamp, and the teaching is light; and reproofs for discipline are the way of life ...

_____

_____

5. What are the some of the benefits of listening to your parents?

_____

_____

THE MAIN THING I LEARNED FROM
EPISODE 5:

_____

_____

_____

_____

CHAMPION SHEET OF DEEDS

Go to the CHAMPION Sheet of Deeds on page 9 and write down one thing you will begin to do before the next session (and beyond) to apply the main things you learned from Episode 5.

EPISODE 6:
A STORM OF DISHONOR

CHAMPION Characteristics
Honor and Attitude

POWER VERSE: ROMANS 12:10

Be devoted to one another in brotherly love; give preference to one another in honor.

Discussion topics:

Show respect to family members

Show honor to others — place value on people and communicate that value to them

Reconnaissance

1. Try to recite all of the CHAMPION Warrior Creed from memory (see page 5).

2. Review the Map of the Mission on page 8 and determine the team's location in episode 6.

3. What is the CHAMPION definition of Honor? Of Attitude? (Refer to the CHAMPION Code on page 6.)

Kind words do not cost much ... yet they accomplish much.

Blaise Pascal

_____

_____

_____

_____

4. How did Pikros and Parakoe treat their father? What did they reveal about their relationship with him?

_____

_____

_____

_____

5. How did Pikros and Parakoe treat each other?

_____

_____

_____

6. How did Teknon feel as he observed the boys' attitudes toward their father? Why did he feel this way?

_____

_____

7. How did watching Pikros and Parakoe affect Teknon's attitude toward his sister Hilly?

_____

_____

_____

8. Do you think Teknon shows respect toward his father and mother? Why do you think so?

_____

_____

_____

_____

_____

STRATEGY AND TACTICS

An Honorable Attitude

Read Exodus 20:12. This is one of the Ten Commandments.

1a. What does this commandment say about the attitude young people should have toward their parents?

_____

_____

1b. What does God promise the results will be if we obey His commandment?

_____

_____

Most of us, swimming against the tides of trouble the world knows nothing about, need only a bit of praise or encouragement – and we'll make the goal.

Jerome P. Fleishman

2. What are some practical ways in which you can show honor to your parents?

_____

_____

_____

3. What does Galatians 6:9-10 say about how young people should treat their brothers and sisters?

_____

_____

_____

4. Read Romans 12:10. How can we "do good" within our family?

_____

_____

_____

The Bible says we ought to "do good to all people." That should especially apply to our family members.

5. How do you view your parents? How about your brothers and sisters? Do you act like Pikros and Parakoe? Or do you view your family, even with their flaws, as valuable people given to you by God?

_____

_____

_____

The members of your family are valuable gifts that God has given you. Are they always easy to get along with? No way! Are you?

Does what they do always make sense? Absolutely not! Does what you do always make sense? Enough said.

A CHAMPION strives to maintain the right attitudes, no matter what other people do. Read Genesis 37:18-36. Joseph's brothers sold him into slavery because they were jealous of him. Even though his capture was a terrible thing, God used Joseph's captivity in an awesome way to eventually place Joseph as the second most powerful man in the Egyptian empire.

Read Genesis 45 to see how Joseph forgave his brothers even when he had the power to hurt them. Joseph understood that "God causes all things to work together for good to those who love God, to those who are called according to His purpose" (see Romans 8:28b).

6. If your brother or sister doesn't show you honor,
    what should you do?

    _____

    _____

    _____

7. Why should you respond this way?

    _____

    _____

    _____

    You should honor your parents as God's chosen
authority in your life. If you have any brothers and
sisters, you should honor them as treasured co-workers
and help your family to become all that God wants it to
be. Don't end up like Pikros and Parakoe. Remember,
you honor God by the way you treat other people.

    Take steps as a CHAMPION to maintain the right
Attitude and show *Honor* to your family.

8. What are some practical ways you can you show honor
    to your mother? How about your brothers and sisters?

    _____

    _____

    _____

    _____

    _____

CHAMPION Sheet of Deeds

Go to the CHAMPION Sheet of Deeds on page 9 and write down one thing you will begin to do before the next session (and beyond) to apply the main things you learned from Episode 6.

Session 4: Episodes 7 and 8 of Teknon and the Champion Warriors

Episode 7: An Excellent Choice

Champion Characteristics

Purity and Integrity

Power Verse: Psalm 101:3

I will set no worthless thing before my eyes; I hate the work [deeds] of those who fall away; it shall not fasten its grip on me.

Discussion Topics

Protect your mind from inappropriate material

Avoid temptation

Run from temptation

Establish your convictions in advance

Reconnaissance

1. Recite all of the CHAMPION Warrior Creed from memory (see page 5).

2. Review the Map of the Mission on page 8 before beginning this section. Identify where the team is located in episode 7.

3. Review the CHAMPION definition of Purity and of Integrity (refer to the CHAMPION Code on page 6.)

_____

_____

_____

_____

_____

_____

_____

4. What did Eros try to get Teknon to do? Why?

_____

_____

5. Why do you think Teknon chose not to stay in the image salon?

_____

_____

6. What did Kratos say about the effect of pornography?

_____

_____

_____

_____

_____

7. Why were Kratos and the mentors so excited about Teknon's decision to leave the imaging salon?

_____

_____

_____

_____

_____

8. Even though Teknon made an excellent choice at the imaging salon, when did he make a bad choice?

_____

_____

_____

Epps helped Teknon to see the danger that surrounded him when he said, "You [Teknon] took a big chance when you decided to go out on your own and walk past those places. All of us are tempted to look at bad material like that, but we can't afford to take those kinds of risks. We've got to stay as far away from them as possible."

STRATEGY AND TACTICS

1. What are some of the sources of pornography in our society? (Hint: Think about what you see and hear.)

_____

_____

2. What do you think pornography does to a person's mind?

_____

_____

Our minds act like computers and cameras. Just as

a computer's response is based on the data programmed into it, whatever data we put into our minds will affect how we view the world and how we respond to it. It's not quite this simple because our minds are far more complex than any computer in the world, but the basic principles work the same way.

You have probably heard the phrase "garbage in, garbage out." When we allow ourselves to view sexually explicit material, it's like downloading a computer virus into the hard-drive of our minds. Those images start to corrupt our thinking and how we react to other people.

Our minds are also like a camera because, when we look at a pornographic picture or video, our minds record it—and store it to be brought back again and again.

> *Failure to prepare is preparing to fail.*
>
> John Wooden

3a. What does Romans 12:2 mean by "do not be conformed to this world"?

_____

_____

_____

_____

3b. What do you think "renewing of your mind" means?

_____

_____

_____

_____

_____

As we choose to draw near to God and yield our lives to the power of His Holy Spirit, He will give us the power NOT to conform to this world. As we allow God to reshape our defective thinking to align with His mind, our attitudes and actions will change. Life-change occurs from the inside out.

4. What do you think this phrase means: "let us throw off everything that hinders and the sin that so easily entangles" (Hebrews 12:1b NIV)?

_____

_____

_____

> *Do not offer the parts of your body to sin, as instruments of wickedness, but rather offer yourselves to God, as those who have been brought from death to life; and offer the parts of your body to Him as instruments of righteousness.*
>
> Romans 6:13 (NIV)

5. Have any of your friends asked you to look at pornography? How did you respond?

_____

_____

6. According to Psalm 101:3, what should your stand be on pornography or any explicit images that tempt you?

_____

_____

7. What does God promise to offer you if you are willing to trust Him when you face a temptation (read 1 Corinthians 10:13)?

_____

_____

_____

Hoplon is a Greek term that refers to armor or weapons of warfare. Just as Teknon and Kratos need their armor to protect them in the battle, Christians also need armor—spiritual armor. The Bible describes this armor of God in Ephesians 6:10-18.

8. What makes up the spiritual armor that God provides for us? How could this armor help you to gain more self-discipline in what you watch, listen to, and read?

_____

_____

_____

_____

_____

_____

_____

_____

These physical objects are metaphors representing God's gifts of protection and spiritual weapons that will help us in the battle against temptation. We need to put on God's full armor or we will not be ready to do battle with Satan. We must trust God and make the right choices in what we see, think, and do.

When you put on the armor of God, it's almost like Kratos putting on the Hoplon. God gives you all of the weapons you need to fight your enemy, Satan. Satan would like nothing more than for you to start a habit of looking at pornographic or sensual material so that your relationship with God and other people will be hindered.

9. What do you think are some of the benefits of not looking at pornography?

_____

_____

_____

_____

_____

PHiL 4:8 STANDARD

Setting high standards for what you watch, read, and listen to is a lot like racing toward that cliff Kratos described a few episodes ago. The best time to put on the brakes is when you know the cliff is ahead. The danger from pornography, like the cliff, is ahead. Decide to put on your brakes now by refusing to look at any pornography. Ask your father or mother, and one of your trusted Christian friends, to pray for you and make sure you are holding the line in this area.

Take heart if you have already failed or even developed a bad habit in this area. Remember that God loves you and is waiting for you to seek His forgiveness. Don't let the guilt that so often comes with this habit overtake you and make you depressed. You can restore fellowship with God today and draw on His strength to help you kick the habit. Jesus said, "I have overcome the world" (John 16:33). Since He has overcome the world, He can help you overcome your habits and tendencies. Be courageous enough to share your difficulties with your father today and ask him to help you.

The Main Thing I Learned from Episode 7:

_____

_____

_____

_____

CHAMPION Sheet of Deeds

Go to the CHAMPION Sheet of Deeds on page 9 and write down one thing you will begin to do before the next session (and beyond) to apply the main things you learned from Episode 7.

Episode 8:
Faced with Fear

CHAMPION Characteristic

Courage

Power Verse: Joshua 1:9 (NIV)

Have I not commanded you? Be strong and courageous. Do not be terrified; do not be discouraged, for the Lord your God will be with you wherever you go.

Discussion Topics

Overcoming fear of rejection and fear of failure

Learning to recover from failure

Optional exercise:
Watch the movie Apollo 13 together

Apollo 13 is an excellent film that describes a true story about facing fear and emerging victorious in what the primary person in the film, Jim Lovell, describes as a "successful failure."

Reconnaissance

1. Review the Map of the Mission on page 8 and determine the team's location in episode 8.

2. Review the CHAMPION definition of Courage. (Refer to the CHAMPION Code on page 6.)

_____

_____

_____

3. What happened to Teknon during the team's fight with the footsoldiers?

_____

_____

_____

> *The credit belongs to the man who is actually in the arena; whose face is marred by dust and sweat and blood; who strives valiantly; who errs and comes up short again and again; who knows the great enthusiasms, the great devotions, and spends himself in a worthy cause; who at the best knows in the end the triumph of high achievement; and who at the worst, if he fails, at least fails while daring greatly ...*
>
> Theodore Roosevelt

4. Why do you think Teknon responded the way he did during the battle?

_____

5. How did Teknon feel about his performance during the battle? Why?

_____

_____

_____

6. Epps also coached Teknon that, "You learn by doing." How does this apply to Teknon?

_____

_____

_____

STRATEGY AND TACTICS

The size of a person is determined by what it takes to stop him. – Dr. Howard Hendricks

Failure has two faces. There are successful failures, and there are unsuccessful failures. *Apollo 13* was a successful failure. Not only did the astronauts return home safely under incredibly difficult circumstances, they also exercised a high level of creative output and genuine teamwork over a period of only five days that rivals any single human endeavor of the century.

Learning to Recover

Dave Simmons, former linebacker of the Dallas Cowboys, had an interesting football philosophy that applies to the rest of life too. He said, "Every play is a game; learn to recover, recover, recover."

Simmons explained in his seminar *Dad the Family Shepherd* that every play during a football game is like a game in itself. The team plans for the play, gets information for the play, and then executes the play. Usually the play is a success. Sometimes it's not. Whether or not the play is successful, the team must come back and execute again.

Let's say it's second down and ten yards to go. The quarterback throws a short pass over the middle. His eyes widen because it's almost intercepted. If it had been intercepted, the cornerback on the other team would have run for a touchdown. After the play, the quarterback is back in the huddle. What's he going to think? What's he going to do?

The quarterback has to do three things. (1) He must learn from his mistake of throwing the ball late. (2) He must decide what he is going to do on the next play. (3) He must recover from the mistake and move on to the next play! The more he plays, the less he will make that mistake again. What would happen if he said to himself, "I shouldn't have thrown that pass; it was almost intercepted. I guess I just shouldn't play football." Nonsense!

There are times when failure is a natural consequence of living. In fact, God often uses trials and failures as a learning process in our lives. When He does this, we learn, as Epps said, by doing. In James 1:2-4 the NIV Bible tells us, "Consider it pure joy, my brothers, when you face trials of many kinds, because you know that the testing of your faith develops perseverance. Perseverance must finish its work so that you may be mature and complete, not lacking anything."

In great attempts, it is glorious even to fail.

Vince Lombardi

If we confess our sins, He [God] is faithful and righteous to forgive us our sins and to cleanse us from all unrighteousness.

1 John 1:9

There are times, however, when we fail because we run from responsibility. Sometimes we run because we aren't prepared for the challenge we face. Sometimes we run because we fear the criticism we might receive from our peers as a result of taking the responsibility. And sometimes we run because we fear the possibility of failure.

Fail, Forgive, and Fortify

Failure can have another name—sin. Sin, simply put, is falling short of God's perfect standard, which results in broken fellowship with Him. Whether we sin by active disobedience or rebellion, or by passive indifference, the result is the same. But we can recover from this type of failure and make it successful.

When we avoid responsibility, we must get back into the game as soon as possible. The recovery progresses in three stages:

I.   **Fail:** We make the wrong decision, do the wrong thing, or find ourselves unable to succeed in a task.

II. **Forgive:** If sin is involved, we seek to restore fellowship with God by asking His forgiveness for our mistake. Then we forgive ourselves for our poor choice and weakness. We also seek forgiveness from people we have hurt.

III. **Fortify:** We recognize God's forgiveness for our failure and His grace for our limitations, learn from our mistakes, and try again.

The Bible describes how the apostle Peter recovered after failing Jesus several times.

1. Check out Matthew 16:21-23. How did Peter respond toward Jesus and his prediction of his own suffering and death? How did Jesus respond to Peter?

    _____

    _____

2. According to Luke 22:54-62, what did Peter do when Jesus was on the verge of being crucified?

    _____

    _____

3. What do you think Peter's responsibility was to Jesus in this situation?

    _____

    _____

    _____

4. Why do you think Peter ran from responsibility and failed Jesus in His time of need?

    _____

    _____

    _____

5. Read John 21:15-19 and Acts 2:38-47. Was Peter able to recover from his failures to obey and follow Christ? How do you know?

    _____

    _____

Peter was one of Jesus' closest friends. In fact, Jesus referred to Peter as the "Rock" because of his faith and strength of character. When Jesus told Peter that all of His friends would eventually deny him, Peter promised that he would never do such a thing. And yet, Peter ran from his responsibility on the night Jesus was crucified. When asked about his friendship with Christ, Peter denied that he even knew Jesus three times!

"What a cowardly failure Peter was!" we might say. How could he recover from such a mistake? He not only sought forgiveness from God for his mistake, but he went on to become one of the most powerful preachers the world has ever known. Peter recovered!

6. Have you ever felt like a failure the way Teknon felt after the battle? Do you think God understands that you aren't perfect?

_____

_____

7. Read Psalm 103:13-14 and 1 Corinthians 1:25-27. What do these verses teach us about our own strength and God's understanding of how we're put together?

_____

_____

> *Even though large tracts of Europe have fallen or may fall into the grip of the Gestapo and all the odious apparatus of Nazi rule, we shall not flag nor fail. We shall go on to the end, we shall fight in France, we shall fight on the seas and the oceans, we shall fight with growing confidence and growing strength in the air, we shall defend our island, whatever the cost may be ... we shall never surrender.*
>
> Winston Churchill (before Parliament in June 1940)

God knows that we make mistakes. He knows us better than we know ourselves because He created us. If you've made a mistake, you can recover. If you've run from responsibility, you can recover. If you've been criticized, you can recover. God has unlimited power to enable you to recover, recover, and recover again. Remember, successful failure is not a bad thing. But if your failure is a sin, you must admit your failure to God, choose not to make the bad choice again, and return to walking with God. If you do these things, He promises to restore you.

8. As a result of what you've learned in this session, how will you handle successful and unsuccessful failures differently in the future?

_____

_____

Do you think that Teknon will learn how to recover and get back into the battle? Press on to episode 9 of the story.

THE MAIN THING I LEARNED FROM
EPISODE 8:

_____

_____

_____

_____

CHAMPION SHEET OF DEEDS

Go to the CHAMPION Sheet of Deeds on page 9 and write down one thing you will begin to do before the next session (and beyond) to apply the main things you learned from Episode 8.

Session 5:
Episodes 9 and 10
of Teknon and the
Champion Warriors

Episode 9:
Recover, Recover, Recover

Champion Characteristics

Courage and Mental Toughness

Power Verse: Psalm 56:3-4

*When I am afraid, I will put my trust in You. In God,
whose word I praise, in God I have put my trust; I shall not be
afraid. What can mere man do to me?*

Discussion Topics

Break out of your "comfort zone"

Be respected vs. liked

Recovering from failure — part 2: don't give in to discouragement

Reconnaissance

1. Recite the CHAMPION Warrior Creed out loud. Pause before you say the lines about courage and mental toughness.

2. Review the Map of the Mission on page 8 to determine the team's location in episode 9.

3. Review the CHAMPION definitions of Courage and Mental Toughness (refer to the CHAMPION Code on page 6).

_____

_____

_____

_____

_____

_____

_____

4. Why did Teknon hesitate to go to the village? What was he afraid of?

_____

_____

_____

5. Why did Tor tell Teknon not to worry about being liked by the Phaskos? What did Tor say about respect? What did he mean?

_____

_____

_____

In the world you have tribulation, but take courage; I [Jesus] have overcome the world.

John 16:33b

6. Look back at episode 4 where Teknon meets the Harpax. Why do you think acceptance by the Harpax was so important to Teknon?

_____

_____

_____

7. What did Scandalon do to Teknon on his way to the village? Why?

_____

_____

_____

8. Why did Teknon respond differently to Scandalon's voice on the way back to the clearing?

_____

_____

9. Why did Teknon want to keep the scar on his arm?

_____

_____

10. Do you think Teknon recovered from his failure in episode 8? If so, how?

_____

_____

Strategy and Tactics

Break Out of the Zone!

Have you ever heard an athlete say, "I was in the zone"? For an athlete, being "in the zone" refers to playing a sport far beyond what he considers his normal ability. If you've had that experience, you know how good it feels to experience that kind of performance. There's another zone, however, that also feels good, but for another reason. It's called the "comfort zone."

You feel good in your comfort zone because life feels easy. The comfort zone is a place where you do things because it's the way you've always done them.

1. Have you ever been afraid to take on a particularly difficult task, or work closely with someone who really seems not to like you, or ask for the help from someone who you're afraid to approach?

_____

_____

We break out of our comfort zone by facing our fears. When we face and conquer fears with God's help, we experience personal, emotional, and spiritual victory.

God Provides the Power to Break Out of the Zone

2. What does King David tell you about who God is and what He does for you in Psalm 27:1,13-14?

_____

_____

_____

Every noble work is at first impossible.

Thomas Carlyle

3. What does Psalm 27:1,13-14 tell you not to do? What does it tell you that you should do?

_____

_____

Breaking Out of the Zone Is Profitable but Not Always Popular

Often, our biggest barrier to break out of our comfort zone is our own fear of what others might say. Nobody likes to be criticized, and nobody likes to be misunderstood. When we do something outside our comfort zone, like giving a speech or sharing our faith in

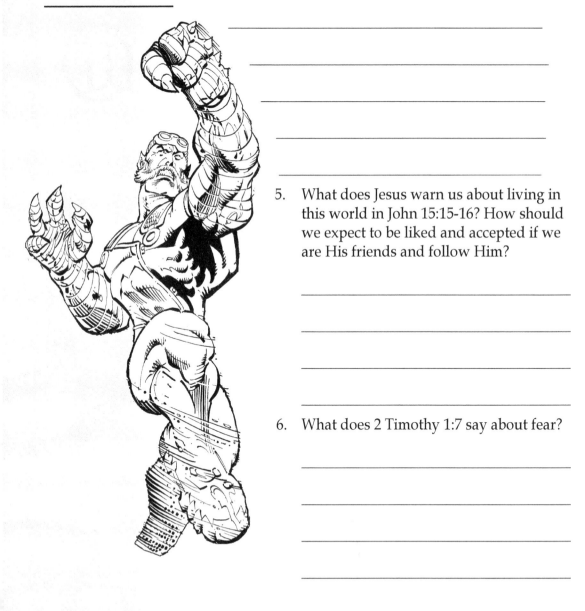

God with someone else, we put our egos at risk. Let's face it: we like to be liked. But it's not necessary to be liked by everyone. At times, people are going to misunderstand us. At other times, people will also become angry with us even when we do the right thing!

> *We all are faced with a series of great opportunities brilliantly disguised as impossible situations.*
>
> Charles Swindoll

4. Read Psalm 56:3-4. If you trust in God, what can others do to you?

_____

_____

_____

_____

5. What does Jesus warn us about living in this world in John 15:15-16? How should we expect to be liked and accepted if we are His friends and follow Him?

_____

_____

_____

_____

6. What does 2 Timothy 1:7 say about fear?

_____

_____

_____

_____

7. What does Jesus say about the truth (God's Word) in John 8:32?

_____

_____

_____

_____

According to Henry Blackaby and Claude King, authors of *Experiencing God*, God is working all around us. When we seek to develop our personal relationship with Him, which began when we invited Him into our lives by faith, He provides opportunities to join Him where He is working. These invitations usually take us out of our comfort zone. But if we step outside the zone (and allow God to accomplish what only He can), we grow as individuals as well as in our relationship with Him.

Breaking Out of the Zone Is Worth the Risk

At times, God asks us to step out of our comfort zone to obey His will. We may not know how we are going to accomplish it, but we know that He wants it done. That's when God expects us to trust in Him by faith and watch Him bring about the results.

8. Read Matthew 17:20. If we have faith in God, what does He say that we can do? How much faith do we need in order to see God do mighty things?

_____

_____

> *Everybody ought to do at least two things each day that he hates to do, just for practice.*
>
> Will James

9. Name three things that would take you out of your comfort zone.

(1) _____

(2) _____

(3) _____

THE Main Thing I Learned from EPISODE 9:

_____

_____

_____

_____

CHAMPION Sheet of Deeds

Go to the CHAMPION Sheet of Deeds on page 9 and write down one thing you will begin to do before the next session (and beyond) to apply the main things you learned from Episode 9.

Episode 10:
Good Enough

CHAMPION Characteristics

Attitude and Integrity

POWER VERSE: 1 Corinthians 9:24-25A

Do you not know that those who run in a race all run, but only one receives the prize? Run in such a way that you may win. Everyone who competes in the games exercises self-control in all things.

Discussion Topics

Pursue excellence

Resist mediocrity

Manage your anger

Reconnaissance

1. Recite the CHAMPION Warrior Creed together from memory (see page 5).

2. Review the Map of the Mission on page 8 to determine the team's location in episode 10.

3. Review the CHAMPION definition of Integrity.

_____

_____

_____

_____

4. Phil said that the Northrons enjoyed mediocrity. How is this revealed in their lives?

_____

_____

_____

_____

5. Tor said that the Northrons "have no vision ... no purpose ... no plan." He said, "Where there's no purpose, there's no passion for living." Why is it important to have vision, purpose, and a plan in our lives?

_____

_____

_____

_____

_____

6. Why did Tor lose his temper?

_____

_____

7. Do you think that Tor had a right to get angry? Why or why not? Was it okay for him to hurt the Northron?

_____

_____

Hold yourself responsible to a higher standard than anyone else expects of you. Never excuse yourself.

Henry Ward Beecher

8. How did Tor feel after he lost his temper? What did he do after he hurt the Northron? Why?

_____

_____

_____

_____

9. What did Epps say was a sign of true strength in Tor? What did Epps mean by that?

_____

_____

Strategy and Tactics

Lukewarm is Not Good Enough

1. Revelation 3:15-16 describes the church at Laodicea. What kind of attitude is Jesus describing here? And what is His response toward this type of attitude?

_____

_____

_____

_____

_____

_____

_____

_____

2. According to Ephesians 5:15-17, how should we use our time?

_____

_____

_____

_____

_____

3. What do you think it means to "make the most of every opportunity"?

_____

_____

_____

> *Average is your enemy.*
>
> Pearce "Rocky" Lane

4. Read Luke 2:40-52. In what ways was Jesus growing as a person even though He was only 12 years old?

_____

_____

_____

God expects us to be thankful for the talents and opportunities He gives us. He also expects us to make the most of the life and gifts He has provided. The story in Luke 2 declares that Jesus grew and kept increasing in stature (physically), in wisdom (mentally), in favor with men (socially), and in favor with God (spiritually). Jesus was a good steward of what God the Father had entrusted to Him. He set an example for us to keep increasing in our maturity by avoiding mediocrity in our lives.

5. In Matthew 19:26 what does Jesus say is possible with God?

_____

_____

6. Read Philippians 4:13. If we are Christians, what can we do as a result of God's power working through us?

_____

_____

USE YOUR HEAD; DON'T LOSE YOUR HEAD!

Do you have a short fuse? When people disagree with you or fail to meet your expectations does your response look something like the fireworks at Walt Disney World? How often do you lose your patience or "blow up" with other people?

It's almost fashionable to have a short fuse, isn't it? Even violent anger is recognized as the status quo.

7. How do you think a person learns to manage anger?

_____

_____

_____

_____

The Bible talks about the process of managing anger as a key component of self-control. Self-control is one of the outward expressions of Christ's presence in our lives as we learn to entrust our lives to Him. The Bible calls these characteristics the "fruit of the Spirit."

8. Read Galatians 5:22-23. What is the fruit of the
    Spirit?

    _____

    _____

    _____

    _____

Uncontrolled anger, like so many other things, can become a habit. Once you get used to "losing your head", it becomes easier to let it happen the next time. Tor developed a habit of losing his temper until he decided to become a CHAMPION Warrior. He knew that self-control was a key characteristic of a CHAMPION and didn't want to accept "good enough" in his life.

If you are a Christian, God expects you to overcome a bad temper by drawing on His power. We plug into His strength by being filled with His Spirit. When you are filled with the Holy Spirit, you start displaying the fruit of the Spirit. It is one thing to hate evil and become angered by its presence in the world. It's another thing to take out frustrations on others. When we do that, we disobey God. If you sense that you have disobeyed God through a fit of bad temper, remember 1 John 1:9 and confess your anger to Him. He will forgive you and reestablish His line of communication and power with you.

But we could spend our lives trying to manage anger after it has erupted. How do we keep from losing our temper ahead of time? The book of James describes an effective formula for anger prevention.

9. Read James 1:19-20. What three things should we do to keep from losing our temper?

Write the formula here:

God's Power + _____ +

_____ + _____

= Anger Management

Keeping our mouths shut is one of the hardest things in the world to do when we get upset. It's also one of the most effective tools in anger management. A spoken word is like a football right before it's intercepted. As much as the quarterback wants it back, he can't get it back. If there is any question whether or not you should say something, DON'T SAY IT!

Instead of being quick to speak, use the other highly effective tool in anger management. Learn to listen. Author Stephen Covey says, "Seek first to understand, then to be understood." Listen not only to what's being said, but also to what isn't being said. Try to put yourself in the other person's shoes so you can better understand his or her position.

God knows that you get angry; He created anger to alert you that something is wrong. But when you get angry, draw on His strength to remain calm and under the control of His Spirit.

Use your head; don't lose your head!

THE Main Thing I Learned from EPISODE 10:

_____

_____

_____

_____

_____

CHAMPION SHEET OF DEEDS

Go to the CHAMPION Sheet of Deeds on page 9 and write down one thing you will begin to do before the next session (and beyond) to apply the main things you learned from Episode 10.

Session 6:
Episodes 11 and 12
of Teknon and the
Champion Warriors

Episode 11:
The Element of Doubt

Champion Characteristics

Integrity and Purity

Power Verse: 1 Thessalonians 5:21-22

But examine everything carefully; hold fast to that which is good; abstain from every form of evil.

Discussion Topics

Know who I am

Identify my personal convictions

Live out my convictions

**Avoid romantic relationships and entanglements
too early**

Reconnaissance

1. Recite the CHAMPION Warrior Creed from memory. If you can, invite two or more people to be in the room when you say it.

2. Review the Map of the Mission on page 8 before beginning this section. Identify where the team is located in episode 11.

3. Review the CHAMPION definitions of Integrity and Purity (refer to the CHAMPION Code on page 6).

_____

_____

_____

_____

_____

4. How did Magos try to confuse Teknon?

_____

_____

_____

_____

Magos wanted to create doubt in your mind about your beliefs, so that you would feel frightened and insecure.

Epps

5. Why do you think Magos challenged Teknon about his beliefs? What did Epps have to say about this?

_____

_____

_____

_____

_____

_____

_____

_____

_____

_____

_____

6. Why did Teknon enjoy spending time with Pary?

_____

_____

7. Describe how Teknon treated Pary during the three days they spent together.

_____

_____

_____

8. After his conversation with Epps, what did Teknon realize that he had done wrong?

_____

_____

_____

9. How did Pary respond when Teknon talked with her that last morning on the beach? Why did she react this way?

_____

_____

_____

10. How could Teknon have prevented this from happening and still maintained his friendship with Pary?

_____

_____

STRATEGY AND TACTICS

1. Read Luke 4:1-13. Who was challenged? — and by whom?

   _____

   _____

2. How did Jesus respond to the temptations and challenges made to Him?

Verses to consider	Temptation/ Challenge	Jesus' response
Luke 4:3-4		
Luke 4:5-8		
Luke 4:9-12		

An expert at anything was once a beginner.

H. Jackson Browne

Jesus was very tired and hungry when Satan challenged His beliefs. But instead of becoming unsettled when Satan tried to use the element of doubt, Jesus quoted Scripture to strengthen his position. He confidently relied on the words of His Heavenly Father.

If you have accepted Jesus as your personal Savior by faith, sooner or later you will get challenged about why you believe in Jesus. If that happens, great! You will have the opportunity to go back to the Bible to find the answers to the challenges given to you. By doing that, you will fuel your confidence and reinforce your position in Christ! If you need help, ask your parents, your pastor, or someone else whom you respect to point you to Bible verses and other Bible-based materials that apply to your situation.

Better yet, even when someone else is not challenging you, spend time reading and studying the Bible now so that you will become more knowledgeable about what it means to be a Christian and apply God's truth each day.

3. Most everyone has asked himself or herself, "What will my friends think if I stand up for what I believe?" Why is that such an important question to us?

_____

_____

_____

Build your character based on what God's Word has to say about His character. Don't get rattled like Teknon. He got stressed out over Magos' challenge, decided to take a break from reality in order to make himself feel better, and hurt himself and Pary in the process ... which leads us to our second topic.

What Does God Have to Say About Relationships?

"Learn to love appropriately. You need to use your head and test your feelings so that your love is sincere and intelligent, not sentimental gush." Philippians 1:9-10 (The Message)

4. It's nice when a girl shows you affection, isn't it? What could be more pleasant than when she calls you on the phone and tells you how great you are? It makes you feel like a million bucks, right? But when you feel that way, whose needs are you meeting — yours or hers? Are you giving in to "sentimental gush"?

_____

_____

_____

Emotions can be weird. When emotions get involved in a relationship between a young man and a young woman, friends start to become more than friends. At that point people often get hurt.

5. Read 1 Timothy 5:1-2. How are you supposed to treat young women if you will honor them and honor God?

_____

_____

6. Is it wise for me to be anything other than a friend to what the Bible calls my sisters in the Lord? Why or why not?

_____

_____

_____

_____

_____

_____

The pressure to start dating and to begin relationships is happening progressively earlier in life. Don't allow yourself to start something romantic that you can't and shouldn't finish. Instead, seek to treat young women as cherished sisters, friends whom you can encourage. Don't get caught up in the gush because there is so much more to enjoy at this point by being friends. This delayed gratification (waiting for what I want until God gives it to me at the right time) will become tougher as the years go by, but God will bless you for making the right decisions. And your effort will be greatly rewarded—beyond whatever you could ask or think! God promises this in Ephesians 3:20. Check it out.

> *The gem cannot be polished without friction, nor man perfected without scars.*
>
> Chinese Proverb

The Main Thing I Learned from Episode 11:

_____

_____

_____

_____

_____

CHAMPION Sheet of Deeds

Go to the CHAMPION Sheet of Deeds on page 9 and write down one thing you will begin to do before the next session (and beyond) to apply the main things you learned from Episode 11.

Episode 12:
Nothing More,
Nothing Less,
Nothing Else

CHAMPION Characteristic

Attitude

Power Verse: 1 Corinthians 15:57–58

But thanks be to God, who gives us the victory through our Lord Jesus Christ. Therefore, my beloved brethren, be steadfast, immovable, always abounding in the work of the Lord, knowing that your toil is not in vain in the Lord.

Discussion Topics:

Manage discouragement

Keep circumstances in proper perspective

Draw on God's strength and wisdom

RECONNAISSANCE

1. Recite the CHAMPION Warrior Creed from memory.

2. Review the Map of the Mission on page 8 and determine the team's location in episode 12.

3. Review the CHAMPION definition of Attitude (refer to the CHAMPION Code on page 6).

_____

_____

_____

_____

_____

_____

_____

4. What were some of the things that contributed to Teknon's discouragement?

_____

_____

_____

_____

_____

5. What, according to Kratos and Phil, is the way to overcome discouragement?

_____

_____

6. Phil told Teknon, "Even when our emotions tell us otherwise, we must stay focused on trusting Pneuma to help us make the right choices." Do you think our emotions are dependable? Why or why not?

_____

_____

STRATEGY AND TACTICS

Many things can cause us to feel discouraged and cause us to start going downhill emotionally. The more we get discouraged and lose hope, the farther down we go. Let's look at several categories of downhills that can cause discouragement.

Category 1: Health Downhills

▲ **Lack of sleep.** Former President Teddy Roosevelt said, "Fatigue makes cowards of us all." If we don't get enough sleep, we can become irritable and start to "cycle down."

▲ **Bad diet.** Too much sugar, caffeine, and fat can wreak havoc on our minds and our emotional stability.

▲ **Lack of exercise.** When we exercise, blood pumps oxygen into our blood and sends hormones called endorphins through our bodies to make us feel alert and energetic. When we spend too much time being a couch potato, we feel and act like sedated slugs.

Category 2: Head Downhills

▲ **Criticism from peers.** Overly critical people can have a negative effect on our attitudes and actions.

▲ **"Successful" failure.** We can become discouraged when we fail at doing the right things, like trying our best but still losing the game.

▲ **Stress.** Too much activity makes us feel like we're under the pile and unable to dig out.

Category 3: Heart Downhills

▲ **Unresolved conflict.** If we haven't reconnected with friends or family after an argument, we will experience a lack of closure until the problem is resolved.

▲ **"Unsuccessful" failure.** When we make a bad choice and disobey God (sin), we will feel miserable.

▲ **Unconfessed sin.** When we don't acknowledge to God that we have sinned and ask His forgiveness, guilt and discouragement will follow.

Teknon's discouragement related to all three of these categories. He was tired and hungry. He had unresolved conflict with Pary. Magos also confused him with criticism of the CHAMPION principles, which caused Teknon to doubt his beliefs and the team's mission. All of these circumstances prompted him to lose hope and start riding the downhill of discouragement.

Until you do what you believe in, you don't know whether you believe it or not.

Leo Tolstoy

1. How might Teknon have avoided becoming discouraged?

   _____

   _____

2. What kind of things get you down emotionally or spiritually?

   _____

3. Is there anything bothering you that you need to discuss? If so, what do you plan to do?

   _____

   _____

There's a lot you can do to dodge discouragement. To avoid the health downhills, you need to eat right, get enough sleep, and get on a regular exercise program. To avoid the head downhills, you should try not to spend too much time with negative people. You should also recover when you have an "unsuccessful" failure, and prioritize your time by involving yourself in only a few activities at a time.

As for avoiding the heart downhills, you should make sure that you are doing what you can to clear up unresolved arguments with others. Most importantly, you need to remember the importance of staying in communication with Jesus Christ. If you have unconfessed sin in your life, the phone lines are cut between you and God. You need to remember how to reconnect those communication lines through confession and turning away from your sin and toward God (repentance).

4. Remember 1 John 1:9? What does that verse say we need to do if we have disobeyed God?

_____

5. What does God promise to do in return?

_____

_____

The longer we ride the downhill of discouragement, the more we take our eyes off the One who can help us. Soon, we start losing hope and forgetting about the big picture. God doesn't want us to become discouraged.

6. You looked at Hebrews 12:1-2 in an earlier session. Look at it again, but this time focus on the first part of verse 2: "fixing our eyes on Jesus, the author and perfecter of faith ... " These verses talk about how we run the race of life that God has marked out for us and how we run to win. What is the big key to

success that you find in verse 2?

_____

_____

_____

_____

7. According to John 10:10, what kind of life does He want us to live?

_____

_____

_____

8. What does "abundant life" or life lived to the full mean to you?

_____

_____

_____

_____

God wants each of us to live a meaningful, significant, maximum kind of life. He understands when you become discouraged, but He also knows that you don't have to stay that way. Take the right steps to get off of the downhill, and start riding the Abundant Life Express transport that God has for you!

The Main Thing I Learned from
Episode 12:

_____

_____

_____

_____

CHAMPION Sheet of Deeds

Go to the CHAMPION Sheet of Deeds on page 9 and write down one thing you will begin to do before the next session (and beyond) to apply the main things you learned from Episode 12.

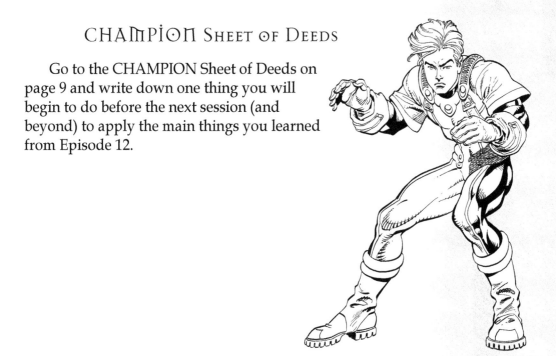

Around the emblem: COURAGE · HONOR · ATTITUDE · MENTAL TOUGHNESS · PURITY · INTEGRITY · OWNERSHIP · NAVIGATION

Session 7:
Episodes 13 and
14 of Teknon the
CHAMPION Warriors

Episode 13: A Job to Finish

CHAMPION Characteristics

Mental Toughness and Navigation

Power Verse: Philippians 3:13b–14

Forgetting what lies behind and reaching forward to what lies ahead, I press on toward the goal for the prize of the upward call of God in Christ Jesus.

Discussion Topics

Choose to focus on the mission

Learn to persevere even in difficult circumstances

Connect with God and draw on His power

Reconnaissance

1. Recite the CHAMPION Warrior Creed (see page 5).

2. Review the Map of the Mission on page 8 and determine the team's location in episode 13.

3. Review the CHAMPION definition of Mental Toughness.

_____

_____

_____

_____

_____

_____

_____

_____

4. Why did Teknon decide to complete the mission on his own after he defeated the amacho?

_____

_____

_____

5. Why do you think Teknon decided to talk with Pneuma?

_____

_____

_____

STRATEGY AND TACTICS

Nobody who ever gave his best regretted it.

George Halas

REMEMBERING THE LION AND THE BEAR

The Bible tells the true story about a young man who completed his mission under very difficult conditions. His name was David. His mission: defeat a 9 foot tall giant named Goliath.
Read 1 Samuel 17:1-54

1. Describe Goliath (verses 4-11 and 43-44).

_____

_____

2. How did David view Goliath (verse 26 and 46)?

_____

_____

_____

3. Why did David believe that he could defeat Goliath (verses 34-37 and 47)?

_____

_____

_____

4. Why did David refuse to wear King Saul's armor (verses 38-40)?

_____

_____

_____

5. What did David use to defeat Goliath (verses 40 and 47-50)?

_____

_____

_____

_____

_____

David was willing to face Goliath because he — a

shepherd boy — remembered how God had delivered him from the lion and the bear in the fields of Israel. David knew that God was watching over him and protecting him.

How to Focus

Let's use David's example to discover some practical steps to focus so that you can accomplish important missions in your life.

▲ **Target your objective.** David targeted Goliath as the adversary he had to defeat for God and his country.

▲ **Train yourself for the mission.** David trained himself both physically and spiritually during his time as a shepherd.

▲ **Think of the resources** you will need to complete the mission. David carefully chose his method and the tools he needed to ensure Goliath's defeat.

▲ **Trust that God will use and empower you** to complete any mission that He has given you. David acknowledged at an early age that his strength came from the Lord.

▲ **Thank God** for His faithful commitment to provide for you so that you can complete the mission. It is very important to remember how God has been faithful to you in the past. David expressed his gratitude to God for delivering him from the lion and the bear and then from Goliath.

▲ **Take action to complete your mission.** David acted upon his trust in God by stepping onto the battlefield. Once he made the first step to confront Goliath, there was

The greatest honor we can give Almighty God is to live gladly because of the knowledge of His love.

Julian of Norwich

no turning back. The Bible says that David actually charged toward Goliath on the battlefield.

It's easy to become distracted from doing the important things in our lives. Sometimes even good things can prevent us from doing the best things — those things that will make the greatest long-term impact. For example, too many basketball games or too much time with friends might prevent us from spending time reading the Bible or finishing our homework.

To become a CHAMPION, you must learn to prioritize your objectives wisely. Then you must focus your mind, your time, and your resources to complete the most important objectives before moving on to the other ones. It won't be easy. But when you look at David you can see the benefits of learning how to focus.

6. What if you don't want to complete an important objective? How do you get it done if you just don't feel like it?

_____

_____

Sometimes you need to have the "want to" when it comes to completing a worthy objective. Sometimes, however, God directs you to achieve an important objective that is not fun or pleasant. If maturity can be identified by your ability to focus, then you show your level of maturity by your willingness to trust God, even through a task that offers little enjoyment throughout the process of completion.

7. Which important objectives do you have that you find easy to accomplish?

_____

_____

8. Which important objectives are tough and demand all the focus you can muster in order to get them done?

_____

_____

THE MAIN THING I LEARNED FROM
EPISODE 13:

_____

_____

_____

_____

CHAMPION SHEET OF DEEDS

Go to the CHAMPION Sheet of Deeds on page 9 and write down one thing you will begin to do before the next session (and beyond) to apply the main things you learned from Episode 13.

Episode 14:
Back to Back

CHAMPION Characteristics

Integrity and Attitude

Power Verse: Psalm 139:14

I give thanks to You [Lord], for I am fearfully and wonderfully made; wonderful are Your works, and my soul knows it very well.

Discussion Topics

**Embrace the strengths and weaknesses
of other people**

**Understand my own unique bent and value
to God's team**

**Harness the power of a diverse team
to complete a mission**

Reconnaissance

It will be important for you to apply all of your "Main Thing" action points after your CHAMPION Training is complete. Over the next few years, you will have the opportunity to develop powerful habits that will advance your development toward courageous manhood. Don't stop the process! Remember what you have learned and continue the process of growth.

Recite your power verse (Philippians 3:13b-14) from episode 13.

Is there an important objective or task that you need to complete? Look again at David's example and the six T's from episode 13. Which of these will help you to focus so you can accomplish your objective? Circle them.

▲ Target your objective

▲ Train yourself for the mission

▲ Think of the resources you will need

▲ Trust that God will use and empower you

▲ Thank God

▲ Take action

Recite the CHAMPION Warrior Creed (see page 5).

1. Review the Map of the Mission on page 8 and determine the team's location in episode 14. They have finally achieved their objective of retrieving the Logos and defeating Magos! But success required tremendous team effort, a great deal of character, and dependence on Pneuma.

2. Review the CHAMPION definitions of Integrity and Attitude.

_____

_____

_____

_____

_____

_____

_____

3. Why do you think Kratos waited so long to let Teknon use his Hoplon?

_____

_____

_____

Tor explained to Teknon what it means to own the mission: "You gained the head knowledge about becoming a CHAMPION, but not the conviction of heart. For that, you had to face the possibility that no one else would retrieve the Logos unless you stepped in. When you did, the mission not only belonged to us, but to you as well."

4. Do you believe God has a mission for you to own? What do you think that mission might be?

_____

_____

5. Dolios transformed himself into Teknon's greatest fear in order to defeat him. What was Teknon's greatest fear?

_____

6. How did Teknon defeat Dolios?

_____

_____

Logos is the Greek term that means "the word." Teknon, his father, and the CHAMPION Warriors risked their lives to retrieve the Logos because of its importance to the people of Basileia. Logos is used in the Bible to refer to thoughts and expressions of God Himself delivered in spoken or written form to us. Jesus is also called the Logos because He is the ultimate expression of God's message to man.

7. Why is God's Word, the Bible, so important to us?

_____

_____

_____

_____

_____

8. Tor said, "There is great power in a team." What do you think he meant by that?

_____

_____

_____

9. Kratos instructed the warriors to "watch each other's backs." Why is it important for us to watch out for each other?

_____

_____

_____

> *Coming together is a beginning; keeping together is progress; working together is success.*
>
> Henry Ford

STRATEGY AND TACTICS

DIFFERENT IS DYNAMIC

It's no secret that we all have different "bents." You may like to be the point person, positioning yourself in front of the group as the leader. Or maybe you like to be in the background keeping track of details and helping get things done. Maybe you're a natural salesman: motivating, promoting, and trying to present yourself well in the process.

Does it bother you that you're not the life of the party? Do you wish that you could make friends easier? Does it bother you that you're a cautious person or don't feel comfortable leading?

The point is this: it takes different types of players to make a great team. God uniquely designed each one of us with different strengths and weaknesses. And it's a good thing that everybody isn't alike. What would the world be like if everybody was a CEO ... or an engineer ... or a salesperson ... or a farmer ... or a public speaker?! In God's plan, different is dynamic. Your unique differences provide a dynamic contribution to the mission God has for His team here on earth. To accomplish an important mission, it takes people with different bents and strengths that can fill in each other's gaps and accomplish more as a synchronized unit than any one person could accomplish alone. Be yourself and bring your unique strengths to your family, your church, or whatever team you are a part of — and make it more dynamic!

How Are You Bent?

1. What do you like best about yourself? What do other people seem to like about you?

_____

_____

Have you ever considered how unique and important your personal traits are in accomplishing God's plan here on earth? Did you know that God designed you specifically with His perfect plan in mind?

2. How well does God know you? (Read Psalm 139: 1-12.) What does He know about you?

_____

_____

3. According to Psalm 139, who created you?

_____

Let us not give up meeting together, as some are in the habit of doing, but let us encourage one another — and all the more as you see the Day approaching.

Hebrews 10:25
(NIV)

4. Describe what Psalm 139: 14-18 reveals about your design and uniqueness in God's eyes.

_____

_____

Do you think God makes mistakes? Of course not! And according to Psalm 139, God made you just the way you are. And because He made you just the way you are, you are fearfully and wonderfully made in His view!

The bottom line: God doesn't want a team made up of clones. God blessed you with a uniquely crafted design for His special purpose in your life. Enjoy the design He gave you and use it to be an integral part of God's team.

THE Main Thing I Learned from
Episode 14:

_____

_____

_____

_____

_____

CHAMPION Sheet of Deeds

Go to the CHAMPION Sheet of Deeds on page 9 and write down one thing you will begin to do before the next session (and beyond) to apply the main things you learned from Episode 14.

Session 8:
Episode 15 of Teknon and the CHAMPION Warriors

Episode 15: Celebration

CHAMPION Characteristics
Navigation and Ownership

Power Verse: 2 Timothy 4:7–8A

I have fought the good fight, I have finished the course, I have kept the faith; in the future there is laid up for me the crown of righteousness.

Discussion Topics

Chart your course and accept your mission

Earn your "wings" so you fly on your own

Celebrate victories and give glory to God

RECONNAISSANCE

1. Recite the CHAMPION Warrior Creed (see page 5).

2. Look again at the Map of the Mission, pause at each location in Teknon's quest, and remember what he learned. Then, review the key things you have learned on your quest for truth. Highlight three important lessons you have learned.

_____

_____

_____

_____

_____

_____

_____

_____

3. Review the CHAMPION definition of Ownership.

_____

_____

_____

_____

4. Why do you think Kratos took Teknon's shield back from him?

_____

_____

5. Why do you think Kratos returned Teknon's shield to him during the celebration?

_____

_____

Kratos is a Greek word that means "power and strength." Teknon means "child" or "youth." During the CHAMPION Training, you have seen how much you should draw from your dad's strength of character and example. Take note that if you also strive to know God and draw on His power, as Teknon did with Pneuma, you will move from childhood toward becoming a young man of character and courage.

6. What did Kratos say to the group about Teknon during the ceremony?

_____

_____

_____

7. Why do you think it was important for the team to celebrate after its victory on Kairos?

_____

_____

_____

8. Why do you think it was important for Kratos to acknowledge Teknon as a young man to his friends and family?

_____

_____

9. What is the team's continuing mission?

_____

_____

_____

Strategy and Tactics

Earn Your Wings

One of the most significant traditions in our country's history is the awarding of a military pilot's "wings." When a pilot has completed his rigorous training, he is invited to a ceremony and presented with a symbol of the rank, skill, and responsibility that he has earned. When he receives his wings, he is authorized to fly missions in the service of his country.

But just because he is awarded his wings, a pilot does not stop training. He knows that he must spend his career logging flight time, learning, training, and growing in his knowledge and piloting skills. He wants to become the best pilot that he can be.

Now that you have completed your CHAMPION Training, it's time for you to receive your "wings" and begin the flight into young manhood.

ACCEPT THE CHALLENGE

Life was different in the mid-1800s. More than a hundred years ago, Native Americans roamed the plains and mountains of the United States. In those days, teenagers became men almost overnight. Young Indian men knew that when they reached a certain age, they were expected to provide and care for a family. They were also expected to join the rest of the warriors from their tribe in battle.

At what age would you be ready to assume responsibility for a family or be willing to fight an enemy to protect your homeland? If you were a Native American during the mid–1800s, you would have been about 14 years old.

But life is quite different for many young adults today. Instead of using their talents and resources to set worthy goals and accomplish great tasks when they're young, they usually settle for trying to get homework done in time to check Facebook. They expect too little of themselves.

You may not be in this camp, especially after finishing your CHAMPION Training. There are young

Bring me men to match my mountains. Bring me men to match my plans. Men with empires in their purpose, and new eras in their brains.

Sam Walter Foss

What kind of man would live where there is no daring? I don't believe in taking foolish chances, but nothing can be accomplished without taking any chances at all.

Charles Lindbergh

adults who make a difference in their families and communities. They remember that God is the ultimate source of their talents and resources. They are thankful for what they have and want to be good stewards. They take responsibility—helping their parents, working hard at school, reaching out to other people, learning what friendship is all about, setting the right boundaries, and so on. These young adults have learned to set high standards for themselves and they are meeting important objectives in life. They seek to know God better and to share Him with others. But remember, there's always room for growth.

10. Review the CHAMPION definition of Navigation.

And looking at them Jesus said to them, "With people this is impossible, but with God all things are possible."

Matthew 19:26

_____

_____

_____

_____

Have you grasped through your training that God has a mission for each of us? Do you realize that He has given you the talents and resources you need to accomplish the mission He has for you? When you use your talents for God, and depend on His power, you are exercising good stewardship. You are becoming God's instrument on earth to accomplish His mission.

So what are you waiting for? Get involved in God's mission as a CHAMPION. Trust Him to accomplish the impossible in and through you, but make sure that you're doing your best to take responsibility to do all that you can to seek God and pursue excellence in every part of your life. Shouldn't you use the abilities and assets that God has given you to accomplish His goals? God's mission will unfold for you day by day if you will commit to follow Him. It's a great adventure!

One more thing ... it's time to celebrate! You've just completed the CHAMPION Training adventure. You've read the episodes, answered the questions, and discussed many topics with your dad. Take time to enjoy this victory and any other victories that you've experienced during your CHAMPION Training. God wants to celebrate the wins in your life and He wants you to celebrate with Him. Thank God for what he has done and for what He will do in and through you as you live your life as a CHAMPION.

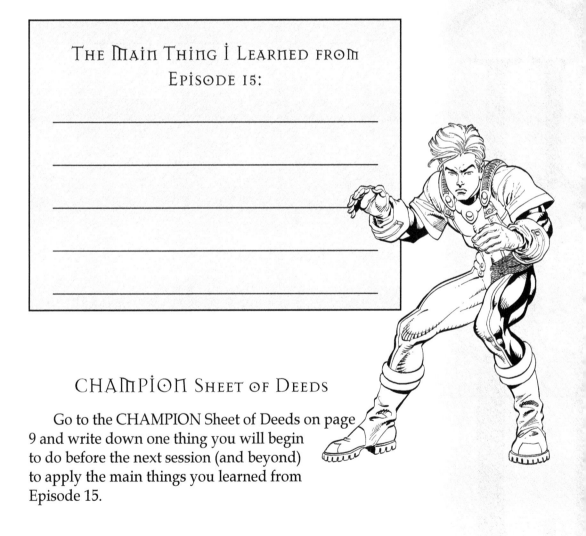

The Main Thing I Learned from Episode 15:

_____

_____

_____

_____

_____

CHAMPION Sheet of Deeds

Go to the CHAMPION Sheet of Deeds on page 9 and write down one thing you will begin to do before the next session (and beyond) to apply the main things you learned from Episode 15.

CELEBRATION CEREMONY

If your dad is planning a celebration ceremony for you, write down the specifics here.

My Celebration Ceremony will be:

Date: _____

Time: _____

Place: _____

Congratulations on a job well done!

Nike® says it, and we buy into it. You look at the "swoosh," as Nike calls it, and the phrase comes to your mind. You hear it in commercials, you see it on the billboards, and it's plastered on millions of shirts, shoes, and shorts. Over a period of time, we come to believe it only because some well-paid marketing wizards found a creative way to sell more products. Now, why don't we say that phrase all together? Ready, one, two, three:

Just Do It!

If only all of life were as easy as this slogan makes it sound. The truth is, life is a lot harder than selling trendy clothing. In fact, we can't "just do it" on our own when it comes to living a life in which we're unconditionally loved, eternally protected, and fully satisfied.

We need power to do that—a lot of power. Power that can only come from an all-powerful God who wants us to relate to Him on a personal level. Only those people who know Him and seek Him have access to God's unlimited power. He offers it as a free gift that we receive through faith in His Son, Jesus Christ.

God created us to have an abundant life now and for eternity. But He did not create us like androids that would automatically love and follow Him. He gave us a will and freedom to choose our eternal destination. What will you choose?

Are you 100% sure that, when you die, you are going to heaven? Why do you say that?

Mark on the following scale how sure you are that you have a personal relationship with God, through Jesus Christ:

Not at all sure   1   2   3   4   5   Very sure

How do you know?

_____

_____

Would you like to be 100% fully sure that you have a personal relationship with God that will guarantee your passport to heaven?

God's power is experienced by knowing God personally and by growing in our relationship with Him. God has provided the power necessary to fulfill His purposes and to carry out His mission for our lives. God is so eager to establish a personal, loving relationship with you that He has already made all the arrangements. He is patiently and lovingly waiting for you to respond to His invitation.

The major barrier that prevents us from knowing God personally is ignorance of who God is and what he has done for us. The following four principles will help you discover how to know God personally and experience the abundant life He promised.

 GOD LOVES YOU AND CREATED YOU TO KNOW HIM PERSONALLY.

a. God loves you.

"For God so loved the world, that He gave His only begotten Son, that whoever believes in Him should not perish but have eternal life."
John 3:16

b. God wants you to know Him.

"Now this is eternal life: that they may know You, the only true God, and Jesus Christ, whom You have sent."   John 17:3 (NIV)

What prevents us from knowing God personally?

2 WE ARE SINFUL AND SEPARATED FROM GOD, SO WE CANNOT KNOW HIM PERSONALLY OR EXPERIENCE HIS LOVE AND POWER.

(Author's Note: The word sin confuses a lot of people. The word sin comes from a Greek term that was used in archery. When archers shot at the target, the distance by which their arrow missed the bull's-eye was called sin. That distance represented the degree to which the archer missed the mark of perfection. When we miss God's mark of perfection, it's called sin too. And because of sin, there is a wall that separates us from a perfectly holy God. Through the years, people have tried many things to break through that wall. Money, power, and fame are just a few of the things people have tried. None of them have worked. We all fall short of God's perfection.)

a. **Man is sinful.**

"For all have sinned and fall short of the glory of God."   Romans 3:23

b. **Man is separated.**

"For the wages of sin is death [spiritual separation from God]." Romans 6:23a

How can the canyon between God and man be bridged?

Jesus Christ is the only provision for man's sin. Through Him alone we can know God personally and experience God's love.

a. **God became a man through the Person of Jesus Christ.**

"But the angel said to them, 'Do not be afraid; for behold, I bring you good news of great joy which will be for all the people; for today in the city of David there has been born for you a Savior, who is Christ the Lord.'" Luke 2:10-11

b. **He died in our place.**

"But God demonstrates His own love toward us in that while we were yet sinners, Christ died for us." Romans 5:8

c. **He rose from the dead.**

"Christ died for our sins according to the Scriptures ... He was buried ... He was raised on the third day according to the Scriptures ... He appeared to Peter, then to the twelve. After that He appeared to more than five hundred." 1 Corinthians 15:3b-6a

d. **He is the only way to God.**

"Jesus said to him, 'I am the way, and the truth, and the life; no one comes to the Father but through Me.'" John 14:6

It is not enough to know these truths ...

4 WE MUST INDIVIDUALLY RECEIVE JESUS CHRIST AS SAVIOR AND LORD; THEN WE CAN KNOW GOD PERSONALLY AND EXPERIENCE HIS LOVE.

a. We must receive Christ.

"But as many as received Him, to them He gave the right to become children of God, even to those who believe in His name."   John 1:12

b. We must receive Christ through faith.

"For by grace you have been saved through faith; and that not of yourselves, it is the gift of God; not as a result of works, so that no one may boast."   Ephesians 2:8-9

c. When we receive Christ we experience a new birth (read John 3:1-8).

d. We must receive Christ by personal invitation.

"I am the door; if anyone enters through Me, he will be saved ..."
John 10:9

Receiving Christ involves turning to God from self (repentance) and trusting Christ to come into our lives to forgive us of our sins and to make us what He wants us to be. Just to agree intellectually that Jesus Christ is the Son of God and that He died on the cross for our sins is not enough. Nor is it enough to have an emotional experience. We receive Jesus Christ by faith, as an act of our will.

These two circles represent two kinds of lives:

Which circle best represents your life?

Which circle would you like to have represent your life?

You Can Receive Christ Right Now By Faith Through Prayer

God knows your heart and is not so concerned with your words as He is with the attitude of your heart. Here is a suggested life-changing prayer:

> Lord Jesus, I want to know You personally. Thank you for dying on the cross for my sins. I open the door of my life and receive You as my Savior and Lord. Thank you for forgiving me of my sins and giving me eternal life. Take control of the throne of my life. Make me the kind of person You want me to be.

> If you sincerely prayed this prayer, you can know with 100% certainty that Christ is in your life and He is there to stay (Hebrews 13:5). So, you don't have to "just do it". God has already done it for you. You may or may not feel like it now, but this is the most important day of your life. To remember this major event in your life when you joined God's family, sign and date this page.

_____   _____

Signature   *Date*

What Are the Results of Placing Your Faith in Jesus Christ?

The Bible says:

1. Jesus Christ came into your life (Colossians 1:27).

2. Your sins were forgiven (Colossians 1:14).

3. You became a child of God (John 1:12)

4. You received eternal life (John 5:24).

5. You have the power to pursue intimacy with God (Romans 5:5).

6. You began the great adventure, the mission, for which God created you (John 10:10, 2 Corinthians 5:17, and 1 Thessalonians 5:18).

Mentor Guide (father's handbook)

Fiction novel

Mission Guide (son's handbook)

CHAMPION
TRAINING ADVENTURE
PROGRAM

For other Teknon and the Champion Warriors resources check out our website at www.ChampionTraining.com for:

▲ Character illustrations and descriptions

▲ Downloadable CHAMPION Creed and Code

▲ Which character are you? personality quiz

▲ New ideas for CHAMPION Training

▲ The Teknon Blog

Acknowledgments

I want to thank my wife, Ellen, for helping me to raise our children. I want to acknowledge my children, Katie, Kimberly, Kyle, and especially Casey for giving me encouragement and inspiration during the creative development of the CHAMPION Training adventure program. Thanks, kids!

About the Author

Brent Sapp lives in Orlando, Florida. When his oldest son, Casey, was nearing the teen years, Brent developed a strong desire to intentionally prepare Casey for manhood. This desire produced many creative mentoring approaches and several key character principles. Brent has adapted these key CHAMPION principles into a futuristic adventure novel for boys. He has also developed an interactive character-building program for fathers to use with their sons as a companion resource to the novel.

Brent and his wife, Ellen, have four children: Casey, Katie, Kimberly, and Kyle.

linkedin.com/in/brentsapp
facebook.com/brentsapp

About the Illustrator

Sergio Cariello is the talented free-lance illustrator behind the characters of Teknon and the CHAMPION Warriors. He also draws such well-known icons as Superman and Batman for DC Comics. In addition, he has taught at the prestigious Joe Kubert School of Cartooning and Animation. Sergio lives in Tampa, FL, with his wife, Luzia.

CPSIA information can be obtained
at www.ICGtesting.com
Printed in the USA
BVHW090050130421
604735BV00008B/722

9 780984 896066